**Copyright © 2023 by Karina G. Sanchez
All rights reserved.**

No part of this publication may be reproduced in any form, or by any means, electronic or mechanical, including photocopying, recording, or any information browsing, storage, or retrieval system, without prior permission in writing from the publisher.

Under no circumstance will any blame or legal responsibility be held against the publisher, or author, for any damages, reparation, or monetary loss due to the information contained within this book. Either directly or indirectly. You are responsible for your own choices, actions, and results.

Please note that the information contained within this document is for educational and entertainment purposes only. All effort has been executed to present accurate, up-to-date, and reliable, complete information. No warranties of any kind are declared or implied. Readers acknowledge that the author is not rendering legal, financial, medical, or professional advice. The content within this book has been derived from various sources.

Please consult a licensed professional before attempting any techniques outlined in this book.

Published by Virago Publishing
www.CorporateToFree

THIS
Journal
BELONGS TO:

Introduction

Starting an online business from home can be a great way for busy women to achieve financial independence and flexibility in their work schedules. With the rise of the internet and e-commerce, starting and running a successful business from the comfort of your own home is easier than ever. As a busy woman juggling work, family, and other responsibilities, starting an online business can be a perfect way to build a career that fits around your lifestyle. This allows you to work at your own pace, set your own hours, and control your own income. However, starting a successful online business does require careful planning, preparation, and execution.

Once you embark on this journey, it's essential to be patient, determined, and ready to learn new skills. This journal will help you set weekly goals, get into the habit of daily reflections on what went well and what could have been done better, will motivate you with weekly inspirations, and encourage you to put your thoughts on paper so that when you look back one year from now, you will see how far you have come.

I encourage you to record your experience, thoughts, feeling, and goals. Always strive to better yourself one day at a time because...

"As long as you don't give up, you can't lose."

When I set out to do this 1.5 years ago, I had no idea what type of impact a simple journal would have on my life. It was life-changing, and I want to do the same for you. So, follow me on this journey, and let's do this together.

Karina G. Sanchez

Begin the Process

How do we define unfounded excuses?

We tell ourselves lies that stop us in our tracks.

Take a few moments to think about what YOUR unfounded excuses are and write them below.

_____
_____
_____

You can do this!

It's time to get motivated.

"Show Me How Good It Can Get"

List some of your own motivational phrases below:

_____
_____
_____

How to create your 'Why'?

List all the reasons why this is important to you. NO judgment; just braindump it all on paper. Once you have an idea, form your "Why Mission Statement."

_____
_____
_____

The reason why I want to have an Online Business is:

_____
_____
_____
_____

My 'WHY' Mission Statement
You 'Mission Statement' will define your 'why' and 'how'.

_____
_____
_____
_____
_____
_____
_____
_____
_____

> *"Change your thoughts and you can change the world."*
>
> ~ Norman Vincent Peale

What You Offer

My skill set and expertise inventory
List all the skills and expertise you have that can be utilized in your business.

All your qualities (ask your friends):

All your qualifications:

All your work experience:

All the jobs you've had:

_____
_____
_____
_____
_____

All the hobbies/passions you have:

_____
_____
_____
_____
_____

Other things you know well or can do:

_____
_____
_____
_____
_____

You must want it and you must be willing to commit.

So... are you committed?

_____

(Yes or No)

Snapshot at the Start

MY CURRENT DEBTS

DATE _____

LIST ALL DEBTS TO BE PAID OFF   DATE TO PAY THEM OFF BY:

○ _____   _____
○ _____   _____
○ _____   _____
○ _____   _____
○ _____   _____
○ _____   _____
○ _____   _____

IDEALLY, YOU WILL BEGIN TO PUT ASIDE 10%-20% OF YOUR PAYCHEQUE. USING "I" STATEMENTS, MAKE A PROMISE TO YOURSELF BELOW TO MAKE IT HAPPEN

_____
_____
_____
_____
_____
_____
_____
_____
_____
_____

AFFIRMATION

*The past no longer matters.
It has no control over me.
I am in total control of my
thoughts and actions.*

JOURNALING...

1st Month

A woman should be two things: who & what she wants."
~ Coco Chanel

PERSONAL DEVELOPMENT

SELF & MENTAL CARE

MONTHLY PRIORITIES

NOTES

Week 1

MY INTENTION FOR THIS WEEK IS...

Your Intention sets the tone for the rest of the week.
Best day to make an intention is Monday morning.

_____
_____
_____
_____

WEEKLY GOAL SETTING

What are your 1 to 2 goals that you will set this week. make them SMART. Specific - Measurable - Achievable - Realistic - Timely

GOAL #1

_____
_____
_____
_____

GOAL #2

_____
_____
_____
_____

WEEKLY GOAL REFLECTION

What did I achieve this week?

What did I learn this week?

What went well this week?

What was challenging this week?

Best moment of the week:

Intentions for next week:

Week 2

MY INTENTION FOR THIS WEEK IS...

Your Intention sets the tone for the rest of the week.
Best day to make an intention is Monday morning.

WEEKLY GOAL SETTING

What are your 1 to 2 goals that you will set this week. make them SMART. Specific - Measurable - Achievable - Realistic - Timely

GOAL #1

GOAL #2

WEEKLY GOAL REFLECTION

What did I achieve this week?

What did I learn this week?

What went well this week?

What was challenging this week?

Best moment of the week:

Intentions for next week:

Week 3

MY INTENTION FOR THIS WEEK IS...

Your Intention sets the tone for the rest of the week.
Best day to make an intention is Monday morning.

_____
_____
_____
_____

WEEKLY GOAL SETTING

What are your 1 to 2 goals that you will set this week. make them SMART. Specific - Measurable - Achievable - Realistic - Timely

GOAL #1

_____
_____
_____
_____

GOAL #2

_____
_____
_____
_____

WEEKLY GOAL REFLECTION

What did I achieve this week?

What did I learn this week?

What went well this week?

What was challenging this week?

Best moment of the week:

Intentions for next week:

Week 4

MY INTENTION FOR THIS WEEK IS...

Your Intention sets the tone for the rest of the week.
Best day to make an intention is Monday morning.

_____

_____

_____

_____

WEEKLY GOAL SETTING

What are your 1 to 2 goals that you will set this week. make them SMART. Specific - Measurable - Achievable - Realistic - Timely

GOAL #1

_____

_____

_____

_____

GOAL #2

_____

_____

_____

_____

WEEKLY GOAL REFLECTION

What did I achieve this week?

What did I learn this week?

What went well this week?

What was challenging this week?

Best moment of the week:

Intentions for next week:

AFFIRMATION

I am a strong, beautiful, capable women, and I too, can do this!

JOURNALING...

2nd Month

"Am I good enough? YES, I am."

~ Michelle Obama

PERSONAL DEVELOPMENT

SELF & MENTAL CARE

MONTHLY PRIORITIES

NOTES

Week 5

MY INTENTION FOR THIS WEEK IS...

Your Intention sets the tone for the rest of the week.
Best day to make an intention is Monday morning.

_____
_____
_____
_____

WEEKLY GOAL SETTING

What are your 1 to 2 goals that you will set this week. make them SMART. Specific - Measurable - Achievable - Realistic - Timely

GOAL #1

_____
_____
_____

GOAL #2

_____
_____
_____

WEEKLY GOAL REFLECTION

What did I achieve this week?

What did I learn this week?

What went well this week?

What was challenging this week?

Best moment of the week:

Intentions for next week:

Week 6

MY INTENTION FOR THIS WEEK IS...

Your Intention sets the tone for the rest of the week.
Best day to make an intention is Monday morning.

_____
_____
_____
_____
_____

WEEKLY GOAL SETTING

What are your 1 to 2 goals that you will set this week. make them SMART. Specific - Measurable - Achievable - Realistic - Timely

GOAL #1

_____
_____
_____
_____

GOAL #2

_____
_____
_____
_____

WEEKLY GOAL REFLECTION

What did I achieve this week?

What did I learn this week?

What went well this week?

What was challenging this week?

Best moment of the week:

Intentions for next week:

Week 7

MY INTENTION FOR THIS WEEK IS...

Your Intention sets the tone for the rest of the week.
Best day to make an intention is Monday morning.

_____

_____

_____

_____

WEEKLY GOAL SETTING

What are your 1 to 2 goals that you will set this week. make them SMART. Specific - Measurable - Achievable - Realistic - Timely

GOAL #1

_____

_____

_____

GOAL #2

_____

_____

_____

WEEKLY GOAL REFLECTION

What did I achieve this week?

What did I learn this week?

What went well this week?

What was challenging this week?

Best moment of the week:

Intentions for next week:

Week 8

MY INTENTION FOR THIS WEEK IS...

Your Intention sets the tone for the rest of the week.
Best day to make an intention is Monday morning.

WEEKLY GOAL SETTING

What are your 1 to 2 goals that you will set this week. make them SMART. Specific - Measurable - Achievable - Realistic - Timely

GOAL #1

GOAL #2

WEEKLY GOAL REFLECTION

What did I achieve this week?

What did I learn this week?

What went well this week?

What was challenging this week?

Best moment of the week:

Intentions for next week:

"Never doubt that you are powerful, valuable and deserving of every chance and opportunity in the world to pursue and achieve your dreams."

~ Unknown

JOURNALING...

3rd Month

"Well-behaved women seldom make history."
~ Laurel Thatcher

PERSONAL DEVELOPMENT

SELF & MENTAL CARE

MONTHLY PRIORITIES

NOTES

Week 9

MY INTENTION FOR THIS WEEK IS...

Your Intention sets the tone for the rest of the week.
Best day to make an intention is Monday morning.

WEEKLY GOAL SETTING

What are your 1 to 2 goals that you will set this week. make them SMART. Specific - Measurable - Achievable - Realistic - Timely

GOAL #1

GOAL #2

WEEKLY GOAL REFLECTION

What did I achieve this week?

What did I learn this week?

What went well this week?

What was challenging this week?

Best moment of the week:

Intentions for next week:

Week 10

MY INTENTION FOR THIS WEEK IS...

Your Intention sets the tone for the rest of the week.
Best day to make an intention is Monday morning.

WEEKLY GOAL SETTING

What are your 1 to 2 goals that you will set this week. make them SMART. Specific - Measurable - Achievable - Realistic - Timely

GOAL #1

GOAL #2

WEEKLY GOAL REFLECTION

What did I achieve this week?

What did I learn this week?

What went well this week?

What was challenging this week?

Best moment of the week:

Intentions for next week:

Week 11

MY INTENTION FOR THIS WEEK IS...

Your Intention sets the tone for the rest of the week.
Best day to make an intention is Monday morning.

_____
_____
_____
_____

WEEKLY GOAL SETTING

What are your 1 to 2 goals that you will set this week. make them SMART. Specific - Measurable - Achievable - Realistic - Timely

GOAL #1

_____
_____
_____
_____

GOAL #2

_____
_____
_____
_____

WEEKLY GOAL REFLECTION

What did I achieve this week?

What did I learn this week?

What went well this week?

What was challenging this week?

Best moment of the week:

Intentions for next week:

Week 12

MY INTENTION FOR THIS WEEK IS...

Your Intention sets the tone for the rest of the week.
Best day to make an intention is Monday morning.

_____
_____
_____
_____

WEEKLY GOAL SETTING

What are your 1 to 2 goals that you will set this week. make them SMART. Specific - Measurable - Achievable - Realistic - Timely

GOAL #1

_____
_____
_____
_____

GOAL #2

_____
_____
_____
_____

WEEKLY GOAL REFLECTION

What did I achieve this week?

What did I learn this week?

What went well this week?

What was challenging this week?

Best moment of the week:

Intentions for next week:

Week 13

MY INTENTION FOR THIS WEEK IS...

Your Intention sets the tone for the rest of the week.
Best day to make an intention is Monday morning.

WEEKLY GOAL SETTING

What are your 1 to 2 goals that you will set this week. make them SMART. Specific - Measurable - Achievable - Realistic - Timely

GOAL #1

GOAL #2

WEEKLY GOAL REFLECTION

What did I achieve this week?

What did I learn this week?

What went well this week?

What was challenging this week?

Best moment of the week:

Intentions for next week:

1st Quarter
DEBT CHECK-IN

DATE _____

LIST ALL DEBTS TO BE PAID OFF | DATE TO PAY THEM OFF BY:

○ _____
○ _____
○ _____
○ _____
○ _____
○ _____
○ _____

IDEALLY, YOU WILL BEGIN TO PUT ASIDE 10%-20% OF YOUR PAYCHEQUE. USING "I" STATEMENTS, MAKE A PROMISE TO YOURSELF BELOW TO MAKE IT HAPPEN

> *"Anything is possible if you have enough nerve."*
>
> ~ J. K. Rowling

JOURNALING...

_____
_____
_____
_____
_____
_____
_____
_____
_____
_____
_____
_____
_____
_____
_____

4th Month

"You have to believe in yourself when no one else does."
~ Serena Williams

PERSONAL DEVELOPMENT

SELF & MENTAL CARE

MONTHLY PRIORITIES

NOTES

Week 14

MY INTENTION FOR THIS WEEK IS...

Your Intention sets the tone for the rest of the week.
Best day to make an intention is Monday morning.

WEEKLY GOAL SETTING

What are your 1 to 2 goals that you will set this week. make them SMART. Specific - Measurable - Achievable - Realistic - Timely

GOAL #1

GOAL #2

WEEKLY GOAL REFLECTION

What did I achieve this week?

What did I learn this week?

What went well this week?

What was challenging this week?

Best moment of the week:

Intentions for next week:

Week 15

MY INTENTION FOR THIS WEEK IS...

Your Intention sets the tone for the rest of the week.
Best day to make an intention is Monday morning.

WEEKLY GOAL SETTING

What are your 1 to 2 goals that you will set this week. make them SMART. Specific - Measurable - Achievable - Realistic - Timely

GOAL #1

GOAL #2

WEEKLY GOAL REFLECTION

What did I achieve this week?

What did I learn this week?

What went well this week?

What was challenging this week?

Best moment of the week:

Intentions for next week:

Week 16

MY INTENTION FOR THIS WEEK IS...

Your Intention sets the tone for the rest of the week.
Best day to make an intention is Monday morning.

_____
_____
_____
_____

WEEKLY GOAL SETTING

What are your 1 to 2 goals that you will set this week. make them SMART. Specific - Measurable - Achievable - Realistic - Timely

GOAL #1

_____
_____
_____

GOAL #2

_____
_____
_____

WEEKLY GOAL REFLECTION

What did I achieve this week?

What did I learn this week?

What went well this week?

What was challenging this week?

Best moment of the week:

Intentions for next week:

Week 17

MY INTENTION FOR THIS WEEK IS...

Your Intention sets the tone for the rest of the week.
Best day to make an intention is Monday morning.

WEEKLY GOAL SETTING

What are your 1 to 2 goals that you will set this week. make them SMART. Specific - Measurable - Achievable - Realistic - Timely

GOAL #1

GOAL #2

WEEKLY GOAL REFLECTION

What did I achieve this week?　　　　What did I learn this week?

What went well this week?　　　　What was challenging this week?

Best moment of the week:　　　　Intentions for next week:

Time for Reflection

Now that you have spent some time journaling and recording your weekly goals, I am sure you have noticed that when you intentionally think about what you want to create, you begin to focus your thoughts on the things that bring you closer to your goal. Each week as you reflect on how much closer you are to building your business and creating freedom in your life, you become more confident in yourself and what you are able to accomplish.

Let me know where you are struggling. What would you like to know more about, what would help you take the first steps towards building your online business.

email me at karina@karinagsanchez.com

"Show me how good it can get!"

~ Unknown

JOURNALING...

5th Month

"A woman with a voice is by definition a strong woman."
~ Melinda Gates

PERSONAL DEVELOPMENT

SELF & MENTAL CARE

MONTHLY PRIORITIES

NOTES

Week 18

MY INTENTION FOR THIS WEEK IS...

Your Intention sets the tone for the rest of the week.
Best day to make an intention is Monday morning.

WEEKLY GOAL SETTING

What are your 1 to 2 goals that you will set this week. make them SMART. Specific - Measurable - Achievable - Realistic - Timely

GOAL #1

GOAL #2

WEEKLY GOAL REFLECTION

What did I achieve this week?

What did I learn this week?

What went well this week?

What was challenging this week?

Best moment of the week:

Intentions for next week:

Week 19

MY INTENTION FOR THIS WEEK IS...

Your Intention sets the tone for the rest of the week.
Best day to make an intention is Monday morning.

WEEKLY GOAL SETTING

What are your 1 to 2 goals that you will set this week. make them SMART. Specific - Measurable - Achievable - Realistic - Timely

GOAL #1

GOAL #2

WEEKLY GOAL REFLECTION

What did I achieve this week?

What did I learn this week?

What went well this week?

What was challenging this week?

Best moment of the week:

Intentions for next week:

Week 20

MY INTENTION FOR THIS WEEK IS...

Your Intention sets the tone for the rest of the week.
Best day to make an intention is Monday morning.

WEEKLY GOAL SETTING

What are your 1 to 2 goals that you will set this week. make them SMART. Specific - Measurable - Achievable - Realistic - Timely

GOAL #1

GOAL #2

WEEKLY GOAL REFLECTION

What did I achieve this week?

What did I learn this week?

What went well this week?

What was challenging this week?

Best moment of the week:

Intentions for next week:

Week 21

MY INTENTION FOR THIS WEEK IS...

Your Intention sets the tone for the rest of the week.
Best day to make an intention is Monday morning.

_____
_____
_____
_____

WEEKLY GOAL SETTING

What are your 1 to 2 goals that you will set this week. make them SMART. Specific - Measurable - Achievable - Realistic - Timely

GOAL #1
_____
_____
_____
_____

GOAL #2
_____
_____
_____
_____

WEEKLY GOAL REFLECTION

What did I achieve this week?

What did I learn this week?

What went well this week?

What was challenging this week?

Best moment of the week:

Intentions for next week:

> "It always seems impossible until it's done."
>
> ~ Nelson Mandela

JOURNALING...

_____
_____
_____
_____
_____
_____
_____
_____
_____
_____
_____
_____
_____
_____

6th Month

"Don't follow the crowd, let the crowd follow you."
~ Margaret Thatcher

PERSONAL DEVELOPMENT

SELF & MENTAL CARE

MONTHLY PRIORITIES

NOTES

Week 22

MY INTENTION FOR THIS WEEK IS...

Your Intention sets the tone for the rest of the week.
Best day to make an intention is Monday morning.

WEEKLY GOAL SETTING

What are your 1 to 2 goals that you will set this week. make them SMART. Specific - Measurable - Achievable - Realistic - Timely

GOAL #1

GOAL #2

WEEKLY GOAL REFLECTION

What did I achieve this week?

What did I learn this week?

What went well this week?

What was challenging this week?

Best moment of the week:

Intentions for next week:

Week 23

MY INTENTION FOR THIS WEEK IS...

Your Intention sets the tone for the rest of the week.
Best day to make an intention is Monday morning.

WEEKLY GOAL SETTING

What are your 1 to 2 goals that you will set this week. make them SMART. Specific - Measurable - Achievable - Realistic - Timely

GOAL #1

GOAL #2

WEEKLY GOAL REFLECTION

What did I achieve this week?

What did I learn this week?

What went well this week?

What was challenging this week?

Best moment of the week:

Intentions for next week:

Week 24

MY INTENTION FOR THIS WEEK IS...

Your Intention sets the tone for the rest of the week.
Best day to make an intention is Monday morning.

_____
_____
_____
_____

WEEKLY GOAL SETTING

What are your 1 to 2 goals that you will set this week. make them SMART. Specific - Measurable - Achievable - Realistic - Timely

GOAL #1

_____
_____
_____

GOAL #2

_____
_____
_____

WEEKLY GOAL REFLECTION

What did I achieve this week?

What did I learn this week?

What went well this week?

What was challenging this week?

Best moment of the week:

Intentions for next week:

Week 25

MY INTENTION FOR THIS WEEK IS...

Your Intention sets the tone for the rest of the week.
Best day to make an intention is Monday morning.

_____

_____

_____

_____

WEEKLY GOAL SETTING

What are your 1 to 2 goals that you will set this week. make them SMART. Specific - Measurable - Achievable - Realistic - Timely

GOAL #1

_____

_____

_____

_____

GOAL #2

_____

_____

_____

_____

WEEKLY GOAL REFLECTION

What did I achieve this week?

What did I learn this week?

What went well this week?

What was challenging this week?

Best moment of the week:

Intentions for next week:

Week 26

MY INTENTION FOR THIS WEEK IS...

Your Intention sets the tone for the rest of the week.
Best day to make an intention is Monday morning.

_____
_____
_____
_____

WEEKLY GOAL SETTING

What are your 1 to 2 goals that you will set this week. make them SMART. Specific - Measurable - Achievable - Realistic - Timely

GOAL #1

_____
_____
_____
_____

GOAL #2

_____
_____
_____
_____

WEEKLY GOAL REFLECTION

What did I achieve this week?

What did I learn this week?

What went well this week?

What was challenging this week?

Best moment of the week:

Intentions for next week:

2nd Quarter
DEBT CHECK-IN

DATE _____

LIST ALL DEBTS TO BE PAID OFF   DATE TO PAY THEM OFF BY:

- ○ _____   _____
- ○ _____   _____
- ○ _____   _____
- ○ _____   _____
- ○ _____   _____
- ○ _____   _____
- ○ _____   _____

IDEALLY, YOU WILL BEGIN TO PUT ASIDE 10%-20% OF YOUR PAYCHEQUE. USING "I" STATEMENTS, MAKE A PROMISE TO YOURSELF BELOW TO MAKE IT HAPPEN

_____
_____
_____
_____
_____
_____
_____
_____

"*Define success on your own terms, achieve it by your own rules, life on your own terms.*"

~ Anne Sweeney

JOURNALING...

7th Month

Life is either a daring adventure or nothing."
~ Helen Keller

PERSONAL DEVELOPMENT

SELF & MENTAL CARE

MONTHLY PRIORITIES

NOTES

Week 27

MY INTENTION FOR THIS WEEK IS...

Your Intention sets the tone for the rest of the week.
Best day to make an intention is Monday morning.

WEEKLY GOAL SETTING

What are your 1 to 2 goals that you will set this week. make them SMART. Specific - Measurable - Achievable - Realistic - Timely

GOAL #1

GOAL #2

WEEKLY GOAL REFLECTION

What did I achieve this week?

What did I learn this week?

What went well this week?

What was challenging this week?

Best moment of the week:

Intentions for next week:

Week 28

MY INTENTION FOR THIS WEEK IS...

Your Intention sets the tone for the rest of the week.
Best day to make an intention is Monday morning.

WEEKLY GOAL SETTING

What are your 1 to 2 goals that you will set this week. make them SMART. Specific - Measurable - Achievable - Realistic - Timely

GOAL #1

GOAL #2

WEEKLY GOAL REFLECTION

What did I achieve this week?

What did I learn this week?

What went well this week?

What was challenging this week?

Best moment of the week:

Intentions for next week:

Week 29

MY INTENTION FOR THIS WEEK IS...

Your Intention sets the tone for the rest of the week. Best day to make an intention is Monday morning.

WEEKLY GOAL SETTING

What are your 1 to 2 goals that you will set this week. make them SMART. Specific - Measurable - Achievable - Realistic - Timely

GOAL #1

GOAL #2

WEEKLY GOAL REFLECTION

What did I achieve this week?

What did I learn this week?

What went well this week?

What was challenging this week?

Best moment of the week:

Intentions for next week:

Week 30

MY INTENTION FOR THIS WEEK IS...

Your Intention sets the tone for the rest of the week.
Best day to make an intention is Monday morning.

WEEKLY GOAL SETTING

What are your 1 to 2 goals that you will set this week. make them SMART. Specific - Measurable - Achievable - Realistic - Timely

GOAL #1

GOAL #2

WEEKLY GOAL REFLECTION

What did I achieve this week?

What did I learn this week?

What went well this week?

What was challenging this week?

Best moment of the week:

Intentions for next week:

AFFIRMATION

I will not compare myself to anyone else because everyone is on their own journey.

JOURNALING...

8th Month

Love yourself first and everything else falls into line."
~ Lucille Ball

PERSONAL DEVELOPMENT

SELF & MENTAL CARE

MONTHLY PRIORITIES

NOTES

Week 31

MY INTENTION FOR THIS WEEK IS...

Your Intention sets the tone for the rest of the week.
Best day to make an intention is Monday morning.

WEEKLY GOAL SETTING

What are your 1 to 2 goals that you will set this week. make them SMART. Specific - Measurable - Achievable - Realistic - Timely

GOAL #1

GOAL #2

WEEKLY GOAL REFLECTION

What did I achieve this week?　　　　What did I learn this week?

What went well this week?　　　　What was challenging this week?

Best moment of the week:　　　　Intentions for next week:

Week 32

MY INTENTION FOR THIS WEEK IS...

Your Intention sets the tone for the rest of the week. Best day to make an intention is Monday morning.

WEEKLY GOAL SETTING

What are your 1 to 2 goals that you will set this week. make them SMART. Specific - Measurable - Achievable - Realistic - Timely

GOAL #1

GOAL #2

WEEKLY GOAL REFLECTION

What did I achieve this week?

What did I learn this week?

What went well this week?

What was challenging this week?

Best moment of the week:

Intentions for next week:

Week 33

MY INTENTION FOR THIS WEEK IS...

Your Intention sets the tone for the rest of the week.
Best day to make an intention is Monday morning.

WEEKLY GOAL SETTING

What are your 1 to 2 goals that you will set this week. make them SMART. Specific - Measurable - Achievable - Realistic - Timely

GOAL #1

GOAL #2

WEEKLY GOAL REFLECTION

What did I achieve this week?

What did I learn this week?

What went well this week?

What was challenging this week?

Best moment of the week:

Intentions for next week:

Week 34

MY INTENTION FOR THIS WEEK IS...

Your Intention sets the tone for the rest of the week.
Best day to make an intention is Monday morning.

WEEKLY GOAL SETTING

What are your 1 to 2 goals that you will set this week. make them SMART. Specific - Measurable - Achievable - Realistic - Timely

GOAL #1

GOAL #2

WEEKLY GOAL REFLECTION

What did I achieve this week?　　　　　What did I learn this week?

What went well this week?　　　　　　What was challenging this week?

Best moment of the week:　　　　　　Intentions for next week:

"Don't give up, don't take anything personally, and don't take NO for an answer."

~ Sophia Amoruso

JOURNALING...

_____
_____
_____
_____
_____
_____
_____
_____
_____
_____
_____
_____
_____
_____

9th Month

"I never dreamed about success. I worked for it."

~ Estee Lauder

PERSONAL DEVELOPMENT

SELF & MENTAL CARE

MONTHLY PRIORITIES

NOTES

Week 35

MY INTENTION FOR THIS WEEK IS...

Your Intention sets the tone for the rest of the week.
Best day to make an intention is Monday morning.

WEEKLY GOAL SETTING

What are your 1 to 2 goals that you will set this week. make them SMART. Specific - Measurable - Achievable - Realistic - Timely

GOAL #1

GOAL #2

WEEKLY GOAL REFLECTION

What did I achieve this week?   What did I learn this week?

What went well this week?   What was challenging this week?

Best moment of the week: Intentions for next week:

Week 36

MY INTENTION FOR THIS WEEK IS...

Your Intention sets the tone for the rest of the week.
Best day to make an intention is Monday morning.

WEEKLY GOAL SETTING

What are your 1 to 2 goals that you will set this week. make them SMART. Specific - Measurable - Achievable - Realistic - Timely

GOAL #1

GOAL #2

WEEKLY GOAL REFLECTION

What did I achieve this week?

What did I learn this week?

What went well this week?

What was challenging this week?

Best moment of the week:

Intentions for next week:

Week 37
MY INTENTION FOR THIS WEEK IS...

Your Intention sets the tone for the rest of the week.
Best day to make an intention is Monday morning.

WEEKLY GOAL SETTING

What are your 1 to 2 goals that you will set this week. make them SMART. Specific - Measurable - Achievable - Realistic - Timely

GOAL #1

GOAL #2

WEEKLY GOAL REFLECTION

What did I achieve this week?

What did I learn this week?

What went well this week?

What was challenging this week?

Best moment of the week:

Intentions for next week:

Week 38

MY INTENTION FOR THIS WEEK IS...

Your Intention sets the tone for the rest of the week.
Best day to make an intention is Monday morning.

WEEKLY GOAL SETTING

What are your 1 to 2 goals that you will set this week. make them SMART. Specific - Measurable - Achievable - Realistic - Timely

GOAL #1

GOAL #2

WEEKLY GOAL REFLECTION

What did I achieve this week?

What did I learn this week?

What went well this week?

What was challenging this week?

Best moment of the week:

Intentions for next week:

Week 39

MY INTENTION FOR THIS WEEK IS...

Your Intention sets the tone for the rest of the week.
Best day to make an intention is Monday morning.

WEEKLY GOAL SETTING

What are your 1 to 2 goals that you will set this week. make them SMART. Specific - Measurable - Achievable - Realistic - Timely

GOAL #1

GOAL #2

WEEKLY GOAL REFLECTION

What did I achieve this week?

What did I learn this week?

What went well this week?

What was challenging this week?

Best moment of the week:

Intentions for next week:

3rd Quarter
DEBT CHECK-IN

DATE _____

LIST ALL DEBTS TO BE PAID OFF

- ○
- ○
- ○
- ○
- ○
- ○
- ○

DATE TO PAY THEM OFF BY:

IDEALLY, YOU WILL BEGIN TO PUT ASIDE 10%-20% OF YOUR PAYCHEQUE. USING "I" STATEMENTS, MAKE A PROMISE TO YOURSELF BELOW TO MAKE IT HAPPEN

10th Month

"There is no limit to what 'we' women can accomplish."
~ Michelle Obama

PERSONAL DEVELOPMENT

SELF & MENTAL CARE

MONTHLY PRIORITIES

NOTES

Week 40

MY INTENTION FOR THIS WEEK IS...

Your Intention sets the tone for the rest of the week.
Best day to make an intention is Monday morning.

WEEKLY GOAL SETTING

What are your 1 to 2 goals that you will set this week. make them SMART. Specific - Measurable - Achievable - Realistic - Timely

GOAL #1

GOAL #2

WEEKLY GOAL REFLECTION

What did I achieve this week?

What did I learn this week?

What went well this week?

What was challenging this week?

Best moment of the week:

Intentions for next week:

Week 41

MY INTENTION FOR THIS WEEK IS...

Your Intention sets the tone for the rest of the week.
Best day to make an intention is Monday morning.

WEEKLY GOAL SETTING

What are your 1 to 2 goals that you will set this week. make them SMART. Specific - Measurable - Achievable - Realistic - Timely

GOAL #1

GOAL #2

WEEKLY GOAL REFLECTION

What did I achieve this week?	What did I learn this week?

What went well this week?	What was challenging this week?

Best moment of the week:	Intentions for next week:

Week 42

MY INTENTION FOR THIS WEEK IS...

Your Intention sets the tone for the rest of the week.
Best day to make an intention is Monday morning.

_____

_____

_____

_____

WEEKLY GOAL SETTING

What are your 1 to 2 goals that you will set this week. make them SMART. Specific - Measurable - Achievable - Realistic - Timely

GOAL #1

_____

_____

_____

_____

GOAL #2

_____

_____

_____

_____

WEEKLY GOAL REFLECTION

What did I achieve this week?   What did I learn this week?

What went well this week?   What was challenging this week?

Best moment of the week: Intentions for next week:

Week 43

MY INTENTION FOR THIS WEEK IS...

Your Intention sets the tone for the rest of the week.
Best day to make an intention is Monday morning.

WEEKLY GOAL SETTING

What are your 1 to 2 goals that you will set this week. make them SMART. Specific - Measurable - Achievable - Realistic - Timely

GOAL #1

GOAL #2

WEEKLY GOAL REFLECTION

What did I achieve this week?

What did I learn this week?

What went well this week?

What was challenging this week?

Best moment of the week:

Intentions for next week:

"You are more powerful than you know."

~ *Melissa Etheridge*

JOURNALING...

11th Month

"Some leaders are born women."
~ Geraldine Ferrero

PERSONAL DEVELOPMENT

SELF & MENTAL CARE

MONTHLY PRIORITIES

NOTES

Week 44

MY INTENTION FOR THIS WEEK IS...

Your Intention sets the tone for the rest of the week.
Best day to make an intention is Monday morning.

WEEKLY GOAL SETTING

What are your 1 to 2 goals that you will set this week. make them SMART. Specific - Measurable - Achievable - Realistic - Timely

GOAL #1

GOAL #2

WEEKLY GOAL REFLECTION

What did I achieve this week?

What did I learn this week?

What went well this week?

What was challenging this week?

Best moment of the week:

Intentions for next week:

Week 45

MY INTENTION FOR THIS WEEK IS...

Your Intention sets the tone for the rest of the week.
Best day to make an intention is Monday morning.

WEEKLY GOAL SETTING

What are your 1 to 2 goals that you will set this week. make them SMART. Specific - Measurable - Achievable - Realistic - Timely

GOAL #1

GOAL #2

WEEKLY GOAL REFLECTION

What did I achieve this week?	What did I learn this week?

What went well this week?	What was challenging this week?

Best moment of the week:	Intentions for next week:

Week 46

MY INTENTION FOR THIS WEEK IS...

Your Intention sets the tone for the rest of the week.
Best day to make an intention is Monday morning.

WEEKLY GOAL SETTING

What are your 1 to 2 goals that you will set this week. make them SMART. Specific - Measurable - Achievable - Realistic - Timely

GOAL #1

GOAL #2

WEEKLY GOAL REFLECTION

What did I achieve this week?

What did I learn this week?

What went well this week?

What was challenging this week?

Best moment of the week:

Intentions for next week:

Week 47

MY INTENTION FOR THIS WEEK IS...

Your Intention sets the tone for the rest of the week.
Best day to make an intention is Monday morning.

WEEKLY GOAL SETTING

What are your 1 to 2 goals that you will set this week. make them SMART. Specific - Measurable - Achievable - Realistic - Timely

GOAL #1

GOAL #2

WEEKLY GOAL REFLECTION

What did I achieve this week?

What did I learn this week?

What went well this week?

What was challenging this week?

Best moment of the week:

Intentions for next week:

AFFIRMATION

I believe in myself and I believe in the path I have chosen. My path will lead to my goals.

JOURNALING...

_____
_____
_____
_____
_____
_____
_____
_____
_____
_____
_____
_____
_____

12th Month

The biggest barrier for women is to think that they can't have it all."

~ Coco Chanel

PERSONAL DEVELOPMENT

SELF & MENTAL CARE

MONTHLY PRIORITIES

NOTES

Week 48

MY INTENTION FOR THIS WEEK IS...

Your Intention sets the tone for the rest of the week.
Best day to make an intention is Monday morning.

_____

_____

_____

_____

WEEKLY GOAL SETTING

What are your 1 to 2 goals that you will set this week. make them SMART. Specific - Measurable - Achievable - Realistic - Timely

GOAL #1

_____

_____

_____

GOAL #2

_____

_____

_____

WEEKLY GOAL REFLECTION

What did I achieve this week?

What did I learn this week?

What went well this week?

What was challenging this week?

Best moment of the week:

Intentions for next week:

Week 49

MY INTENTION FOR THIS WEEK IS...

Your Intention sets the tone for the rest of the week.
Best day to make an intention is Monday morning.

WEEKLY GOAL SETTING

What are your 1 to 2 goals that you will set this week. make them SMART. Specific - Measurable - Achievable - Realistic - Timely

GOAL #1

GOAL #2

WEEKLY GOAL REFLECTION

What did I achieve this week?

What did I learn this week?

What went well this week?

What was challenging this week?

Best moment of the week:

Intentions for next week:

Week 50

MY INTENTION FOR THIS WEEK IS...

Your Intention sets the tone for the rest of the week.
Best day to make an intention is Monday morning.

WEEKLY GOAL SETTING

What are your 1 to 2 goals that you will set this week. make them SMART. Specific - Measurable - Achievable - Realistic - Timely

GOAL #1

GOAL #2

WEEKLY GOAL REFLECTION

What did I achieve this week?

What did I learn this week?

What went well this week?

What was challenging this week?

Best moment of the week:

Intentions for next week:

Week 51

MY INTENTION FOR THIS WEEK IS...

Your Intention sets the tone for the rest of the week.
Best day to make an intention is Monday morning.

WEEKLY GOAL SETTING

What are your 1 to 2 goals that you will set this week. make them SMART. Specific - Measurable - Achievable - Realistic - Timely

GOAL #1

GOAL #2

WEEKLY GOAL REFLECTION

What did I achieve this week?

What did I learn this week?

What went well this week?

What was challenging this week?

Best moment of the week:

Intentions for next week:

Week 52

MY INTENTION FOR THIS WEEK IS...

Your Intention sets the tone for the rest of the week.
Best day to make an intention is Monday morning.

WEEKLY GOAL SETTING

What are your 1 to 2 goals that you will set this week. make them SMART. Specific - Measurable - Achievable - Realistic - Timely

GOAL #1

GOAL #2

WEEKLY GOAL REFLECTION

What did I achieve this week?

What did I learn this week?

What went well this week?

What was challenging this week?

Best moment of the week:

Intentions for next week:

4th Quarter
DEBT CHECK-IN

DATE _____

LIST ALL DEBTS TO BE PAID OFF	DATE TO PAY THEM OFF BY:
○	
○	
○	
○	
○	
○	
○	

IDEALLY, YOU WILL BEGIN TO PUT ASIDE 10%-20% OF YOUR PAYCHEQUE. USING "I" STATEMENTS, MAKE A PROMISE TO YOURSELF BELOW TO MAKE IT HAPPEN

_____
_____
_____
_____
_____
_____
_____
_____
_____
_____

AFFIRMATION

I will award and praise myself for my accomplishments. I deserve good things in my life and I work towards my success.

JOURNALING...

Conclusion

This is it! You know what you need to do. There is no more wondering in the dark. You can trust yourself because now this information is ingrained in your mind, deep in your mind. You can do these check-ins every time you need them and you can set your weekly goals all by yourself now. I believe in you and you need to believe in yourself.

The world is your oyster. You find your pearl. Be bold, persist and you will achieve your goals. I know this like I know that life is what you make it, so make it the best one you will ever have!

> *"You'll never do a whole lot unless you are brave enough to try."*
> ~ Dolly Parton